BECAUSE THE BRAIN CAN BE TALKED INTO ANYTHING

BECAUSE THE BRAIN CAN BE TALKED INTO ANYTHING

POEMS BY JAN RICHMAN

LOUISIANA STATE UNIVERSITY PRESS
BATON ROUGE AND LONDON

1995

Designer: Glynnis Phoebe
Typeface: Display, Copperplate 33bc; text, Bodoni
Typesetter: Moran Printing, Inc.
Printer and Binder: Thomson-Shore, Inc.

Library of Congress Cataloging-in-Publication Data
Richman, Jan.
    Because the brain can be talked into anything : poems / by Jan
Richman.
        p.   cm.
    "Walt Whitman award winner"—Data Sheet.
    ISBN 0-8071-1993-8. — ISBN 0-8071-1994-6 (pbk.)
    I. Title.
PS3568.I3504B43   1995
811'.54—dc20   94-37532
                                                     CIP

Grateful acknowledgment is made to the editors of the following periodicals, where some of the poems in this manuscript originally appeared, sometimes in slightly different form: *Ark* (1988), "Night Flight, California"; *Black Swan Review* (1990), "You've Changed, Dr. Jekyll," "The Devil's Advocate Threatens the Devil"; *The Bloomsbury Review* (Winter, 1982), "Tecolutla, 3 A.M.," (Spring 1994), "The First"; *Bluff City* (1992), "Greetings from Quartz Canyon," "Letter to Jeanne"; *Caliban* (1991), "History," (1992) "Drug Stories"; *Five Fingers Review* (1987), "Parting the Waters"; *The Madison Review* (1991), "Hells," (1993), "Belief System," "Joint Venture," "Grace"; *Nation* (May 3, 1993), "The Physics of Dating"; *Negative Capability* (1995), "Cancer, My Mother's Face"; *Nimrod* (Fall/Winter, 1993), "The Gape"; *On Our Backs* (March/April, 1991), "Lila"; *Ploughshares* (Winter, 1993–94), "Ajijic," "Origami for Adults"; *Transfer* (Fall, 1982), "Fairy Tales"; *ZYZZYVA*, (Fall, 1994), "Rockabye."

Publication of this book has been supported by a grant from the National Endowment for the Arts in Washington, D.C., a federal agency.

**WINNER OF
THE
WALT WHITMAN AWARD
FOR 1994**

Sponsored by the Academy of American Poets, the Walt Whitman Award is given annually to the winner of an open competition among American poets who have not yet published a first book of poems.

Judge for 1994:
Robert Pinsky

I'd like to thank my father and Roger and Beverly Richman for their generosity and support during this book's long genesis. Many thanks also to Jane Ransom, Robert Kendall, and Robert Pinsky for their fierce attention and diagnostic advice.

Contents

I

REASONS

HELLS

Everyone has gone through hell, that's
what I love about the world. Even dentists,
and the couple in the convertible thrilling
Central Park West, winter lights landing
like spacecraft on their hair. In the dark
under the dashboard, their shoes
pinch their feet unflaggingly.
Babies knew hell, and judges, and Merlin, and nuns,
especially nuns. There is the hell of the loyal
fan, the hell of the germ, and of the arm
that reached so far across the fence
that it's become the fence. Just think
of the not-yet-born, those poor wanderers
without organs or bills of health to fear for,
scouting out the helicopter with its rhythmic slashes.
Sometimes I rejoice when my body greets me
at the corner, saying Hello I'll be your ride
home tonight, and I aim for the wig
of that body talking, gratefully climb
into its pathetic skin, as into
the consolation of the specific.

WHY I'M THE BOSS

Because I'm tired of being alarmed by steam gushing
from invisible openings all over the city, like bodies
of culture in a dark age, tired of freezing
at the sight of a wound devouring itself with blood,
tired of imagining life as a game show with an off-screen
panel of experts, smoking and holding up numbered cards.
Tired of waiting in waiting rooms for a chemical
to tell me the meaning of my morning sickness.
Tired of being sucked out of the night sky
to be handed books on astronomy.

Because look how far my ancestors got after shedding
and carefully folding their clothes.

Because no, I wouldn't trust Jesus if he rose and ran
for president, or Buddha, or Mohammed; I wouldn't open my legs
for Saint Francis himself. In this sense, I am truly
an American. A pilgrim, even. Spliced from one of those
who died on the journey, and one who lived to yell, "Timber!"

Because I've bowed to my elders in cemeteries and putting greens,
card rooms and customer-service lines, bowed to clank
with other bowing heads, bowed to television, and letters
after my name, to weddings and lie-detector tests.

Because the brain can be talked into anything.
Because I alone can perfectly forge my signature,
and my own hot tongue's stamp of approval.
Because the center of my belly is a puckered wound
that pours curse like steam with the effort
of forgetting, or quite remembering, its source.

HISTORY

When they teach history, they never say that the sky was always
old and worn thin, delicate as an heirloom breathing the light
of many past loves, and that people were relieved, after talking
with a friend or biting into another bitter hunger, to look up
and find it.

When they say Napoleon was a greedy man, they never say like your
father is a greedy man, the fever in his eyes clotting you out
of the picture while his mouth sucks at your barely breast and
his tongue curls around the sacred mound of ownership. Like you
are a greedy man, though you are empty, and not a man.

When they circle words to remember, they don't tell you this paper
will self-destruct before you can plan a revolution, that the life
of a book is a dream leapt from a sudden doorbell, that time is a cat
who is always sharpening her claws, waiting for you to arrive.

Do it yourself: unbundle your ancestors at the end of their wits
who keep your blood in your veins. Slice your paper doll from her
faded background and wear her like a bridal veil, a graduation gown,
a death shroud. History is memory, and it is gone, and it is here
coating the tip of your next words.

GOLD BALL FALLING

Thin motel drapes half-maim the highway world. Cars are severed from their shadows, and the thrill of solid approach gets scattered. How many nights happened before this one, nights that didn't include me? She lies facing the mirror, and her reflection is dizzy with dark, deformed by it. You could almost believe that the woman in the mirror sleeps, but the breathing from the bed is too quiet; it intrudes on the air. He lies next to her, twitching. I can't tell where his eyes look. I can smell him across the night table, toothpaste and whiskers. He hasn't wanted me for a while. The flicker of headlights, like a home movie, patterns his legs for an instant. His head, out of range, stays buried in its separate pocket. I slowly lower the elastic neckline of my nightgown until one small white breast glimmers into the room. White gold against the average blue of adventure. A river raves in through the window, drawn like insects to light. I remember, I remember. Unmistakable. How does it feel to lose everything? A gold ball falling through murky space, so heavy and valuable all it can do is fall. The ceiling swarms. My father is snoring.

TECOLUTLA, 3 A.M.

I was eight when I first saw the night.
Ripped from a dream, upholstery was awake
under me. The awful heat was like a mother's handclasp.
A fossil of spit clung to the window,
white against the bigger white of the station.
I reached across with my bare leg,
squeaked the length of the sweating seat, its deep
mouth full of sandals and suitcases.
Splintering bandbox beneath my father's shaving kit, and
me on top, shirtless Mexicans
playing cards on stained cement,
my mother far away, holding a Pepsi against her cheek.
Behind them, blackness with my face stenciled on it.
Blackness so big I couldn't see over it.
I pushed the window down into its crusty metal.
My hand slid through the fever-air
and touched, carefully, the pulsating train.

AJIJIC

The lengthy lawns of the rich run down
to the lake's lap. Cats steal *chiroles* from the nets
where they're drying on the shore. Dresses and jeans
lie flat below the fish, dancing an ancient, static line.
Their owners' hair floats in black, soapy masses
on the green sway. I'm stuck in jangling shade, no matter
where I walk, bored as a horse, flies in my vision.
The naked babies are held up, glistening brown.
At the lakeside café, Americans eat *seviche*
with tan, silvered hands. I came down to the water
to escape the feuding, infallible generations.
In my grandfather's eye is my father's eye, and so on.
There'll be green mango pie and tequila for supper.
The trucks will sing on the highway all night.
These clean girls will circle the plaza clockwise,
entwined in pairs, throbbing to be plucked from the wheel.
I'll dance in the bar with Mexican boys
who'll squeeze my ass and tell my white throat, You,
alone, are beautiful. The clothes pale as they dry,
the *chiroles* darken. A small girl throws sand
at the boldest cats and chatters, rolling her eyes.
They meet mine, then bolt away, as though
I could infect her with my gaze, unfasten her
from her familiar, exacting chore.
As though if I could, I would.

BELIEF SYSTEM

My grandfather is an atheist from way back.
The name of his winter is not something you could carve
in your mailbox or sing about, but more like the red ant
who keeps dying in your jeans. A phantom itch. Not
a symbol. Life has disappointed with its flagrant self-love.
My grandfather bit off his own glory long ago
on his way to get a haircut. He barrel-stared a tight lane
of buildings gone cornflower blue by the light (and when
he stared it was like he was fly casting,) turned
with the blue to gold then grey, decided then and there
we are not made in the image of anything fickle, anything
that requires a cut and a shave. The alchemy
of this sun's flight pattern takes a truly dry eye
to perceive.

Nah, I made that up. I'm trying to believe he doesn't
think he's God.

He believes it. Like the objective scientist wants to cure
or not cure cancer. I used to go to Sunday school
just to piss him off. "What does she need that crap for?"
Need lifts its arms and carries the sentence.

My grandfather is a card shark.
He doesn't let luck take up any slack; he simply
never looks away. I make a scorecard
in the sand, late, exaggerating each grainy kiss,
drawing out the spidery mathematics like a long life
right up to the water's lip. In the morning it'll be gone.
He lies awake, I think, in the foreign language
of night, bluffing sleep and bargaining shrewd
contracts with his hard, refusing eye. It's not that he's
afraid to die; he doesn't like the turbulence of dreaming.

PARENTS

The woman, when she nods, creates a small
clearing for herself beneath the stars, a state
of temporary grace. Now the phone won't ring
during dinner. The kids will hear each other's reasons.
He'll want to become her, and she'll concede,
wanting to become invisible. His fingers,
ten viruses, will pan her blood for gold.
But he can't hold such concession, such soft soil;
it sifts right through him glittering.

Other times, though, she just can't stand him.
Even his car in the driveway is a stone in her lung.
She squints, charting the odds for survival
in the wilderness. Knotted nights like these, he holds
up a plate till she sees herself: Look what you've come to.
Busy, busy. *Who* do you hate? What she could say
pales inside the bright void her absence would create.
It's the spotlight that needles them.
It's the possibility they both live by.

THE FIRST

The first person who ever ate an orange
ate the peel. That's why love's so compelling, its
mainspring perpetually rigged up and ready to roll,
electing *you*: Yo! Recipe-maker! Food-taster! Saint of first
causes! Bring your whelp of a tongue over here.
Passion's eyes say nothing of the string of goods
changing hands behind. Waves break their backs
over law-abiding currents, while a smooth skin of sand
sings bed over a restless hot-fisted earth.
This is life, is all. It is the circle the saw makes.
Even death is penetrable, but watch that yawning
loophole. A canary dips into the mine shaft and breaks the
news, makes the news, carves out its peerless by-line. Yes,
the first mortal must have felt something like joy
when she unfolded her crowning assignment.
Her limbs' sudden weight tearing a sigh from lucid air,
and the peopled frame tightening, tightening as she moved,
there must have been a lively, insistent churning:
I, I.

CANCER, MY MOTHER'S FACE

Cancer, my mother's face, the great
vacuum of the brain, black hole
pulling everything toward it,
bone-shadow easing its final shapes
onto the same skin of her childhood,
her legs like a young girl's—skinny
and white and bare. I knelt
by this woman who didn't love the world—
not prayer exactly, but memorization:
her hands, long and deliberate, the only
part of her that always seemed
to belong to whatever she did,
her eyes poisoned, tainted by blue.
She didn't really know me; we didn't
have words; everything was new.

THE GAPE

Each crow follows the black point ahead
in the corner of his vision. This affords him
both the arrogance of brotherhood and the distance
to speculate on dinner. If it seems
beautiful, if it reminds you of a necklace
unlatched and flung, of the intimate
and frail order of things, that is purely
accidental. A stark, round baby
may think murderous thoughts. If to lurk
and to reside were synonymous, we'd be making
new mistakes instead of the same old ones.
Often, what you think you hear improves on
what you hear. For instance, when my mother died,
we couldn't close her mouth. Three of us trying.
First with pillows, lifting and propping.
And finally, alone, I had her down, tackled,
her whole head tucked in my arm like a nut,
and as I wrestled and pried, imagining the civic
clack of teeth, I thought I heard the ocean
in that dry, ancient cave, rinsing my ear,
I thought I heard the violence of sand.

GREETINGS FROM QUARTZ CANYON

Everyone, bite down on the bitter pill of beautiful
backyard living. Click. My brother greets the guests,
his pain voraciously prisoned, like a bright
quarter, between his eyes. A death
and a death wish size each other up, shrunken head
on a plate of cocktail franks.

His wife's smoking crack with a brutal,
tender-when-drunk gas station attendant,
but we don't know that yet. I sit in the back
bedroom on a launching pad and call my life collect.
My brother scans his reflection for a trace
of emergency; I wave; he doesn't see.

Our mother's ghost checks the backs of her legs
for lawn chair tattoos. I still don't know
what she's thinking. If I had a drink
I could emerge and ask my father for a drink.
He sweats and gestures, as if explaining
to a hung jury his stainless motives.

Coyotes will stalk the patio tonight when the lime
blossoms prosper and a quartz moon pales the sky.
I used to sit up in bed for their invasion—
a rankness too passionate for the suburbs,
their black silhouettes riding the skyline like boxcars
on the edge of a brilliantly landscaped eyesore.

TOURETTE'S JOURNEY

Shudder and sigh, fuck fuck fuck, stutter
and thwack the roof of the car, knuckles
calloused and winking, each tin pop a delight,
then swing to strike again, think of nothing
but the bright pang of your body knocked against
the rollicking world, eyes banged shut
like a doll set in motion, poke at your balls
till you feel the rush swerving off you like steam
off a fresh pile of shit.

Check the speedometer. Hands on the wheel.
Ask your wife if she's thought about dinner
or whether it matters your spare pair of glasses
lies bent by a heft of mail on the kitchen
counter. For her, the world is flat. Pat
her thigh. A margin of bottlebrush pitches by
on the right, blooming pinch-red bristles onto the
outside lane. You know this road so well
a river of shame wouldn't surprise, too
well, ice and eyes.

Her thighs are warm as kettles, your palms moist
as hiss, a calm discontent falls down
like a bucket from a balcony, luck and piss
and sweat and boil offer up most of their honey-
tongued tricks. Crack your window, slap the pane
that separates this chestnut hush from that
parenthetical strain. Shit it's good to brain
something, to be clashed and parried, pummeled
into a different meaning, shifted into distress,
breastplate gleaming, god damn, god fucking
damn, and god bless.

You've Changed, Dr. Jekyll

My, what big teeth you have. And I can't help but notice
your inseam sneak up to your chin and beard your uncircum-
stance. Your lace collar shudders, and . . . Now you remember:
Smile, an ordinary word. Chat. Beat. Brag. While your left hand
conducts an under-the-table ejaculation, your right
flips the rusty tongue of a Dream Date lunchbox, airing
its contents: laboratory mythologies. Yawn. Why do
historical men either gorge or starve? Come midnight,
you'll paint the town red, your lips wrapped around
a block-long siren, greased and bawling like a burned baby.
Now you're in the parlor deciphering forgeries.
Good eye. But what's that stain? You're due at the Nobels'
for dinner in an hour. Herr Doctor, Mr. Dad, you've handed
down a scratchy decree, this cushion on which I sit to jerk
off in the meager poem of your hiding place. Five hot minutes
on the phone with legacy equals a cup of serum. Hallelujah!
Accepting the award for Mlle. Hyde is cultured silence
braying like a Baptist: Oh yes, I can love all things,
just not at the same time.

ACTING OUT

My laugh is like a beefsteak, my
temperature is zero. On the gills
of my dodge the inscription reads fast
and easy like an espionage thriller
or a frictional fuck. 3-in-1 oil and 2 wrongs
make a right. It's true, it's better
to be funny than funereal. A chuckle in the hand
is worth a bushel of concerned couch
doctors dressed in pearls.

The only thing that matters is how
you slice it. The sunset gradations of pink
we love so well appear in all rare meat.
The art is in presentation.
Primal scenes are boring; let me
tell you my dreams. Or would you like a bite
of the banana flambé I made instead
of murdering my father?

Once upon a time I could drop
a blotter, lie down on a freezing
marble slab downtown at dawn and imagine
getting fucked by a building. Let's face it,
men's erections have always left me
cold. And hotheaded. Feed my journals to the dog,
my mother was a saint. My epitaph: The best jokes come
to those who wait.

There are so many. The one on the roof
throwing brilliant flounders like animal fire
back to the bay, round ripples licking their lips
all the way to sunrise. Or the raccoons at the file
cabinet, shuffling through bank statements, looking
over their hunched, criminal shoulders. There was Daniel
dreaming of fucking his own corpse. And rinsing our hair
under one faucet—black dye, green dye, red dye,
yellow dye, blundering like dumb snakes
down the sewers. I met myself at puberty,
then carried my baggage farther on, nodding to that
wizened train companion, Oriental spy, memorizing
the fond hairs on her chin. That's the time we dove
off the Holiday Inn, naked down to our tail-
feathers, footmarking the sky for a pack
of shocked tourists, turned-up and land-bound
as mushrooms. Calling many names: bum, failure, freak,
comrade. We were stirring it up on the pavement,
brandishing our coats of mud and lime,
laying down our stretch of road, our curve. Romping
in bus seats, slapping the faces of walruses
all along the beach. I saw a ship sink, a fire gorge,
a person's mind change. I thought being in love
was talking someone down a bad trip. And it's true.
Now we never step into each other's metaphors,
wring out the safety, bear witness to all the deities
under the skin, and emerge plainly poisoned,
but poisonous too.

Rain's preaching again. Won't take no
for an answer. I don't mind the bee sting,
riptide, take-it-home rhythm, come and get it,
came and hear your handsome pony calling,
like shooting arrows one after another
and feeling them climb your vertebrae.
But I'm not listening to more stories
about big teeth heroes with their hands
hanging out. Bounce with the ball until you're
monkey dancing with a sheet over your head.
Any volunteers? The roof's shredding like
newspaper, and whole crops are aimless.
Pitter patter is nature bragging
about the size of her womb.
Jackknife thunder is the timeless sound
of God dropping his enormous seed
onto a tiny, handcuffed audience.

I was conceived in the blue light
of Johnny Carson's personality.
I traded all my Granny Smiths
for candy. The moon is a place
to send picture postcards back from.
The curve in a river is nothing
but a sound effect. I know
anything's possible, eye-level
sublime with ears for bending.
I didn't bargain for handshakes.
I wasn't around before diplomats.
But the smell of perfume travels
to the whitest chamber in my brain,
ringing a bell.

Rain's preaching again, but no one here
needs saving. Go ahead, wet the bed,
blow the windows out of their sockets,
show me how your palm could smother me

with one good squeeze. Black out
the buffalo range. Shock the candelabrum.
Shiver open my cupboards, no congregation
this thankless body stacked with breakables.
I already heard the one about the dead
getting back up on their saddles.
Men ten times my size pop up
everywhere I look and all of them
got gum-cracking smiles.

There's a song I remember from before
I was born, and it goes like a mouth
that's never been kissed, a big blue bowl
with a marble in it that keeps rolling
with no place to stop, a ten-story rainbow
with one color missing. Even the chirp
of water can send me packing. Because
floating on the flood are a thousand books,
all balanced on their spines, wagging their
tongues, hiding their soggy, swollen names.

WHO AM I?

Ask my bank, or my congressman.
Ask UPI for stats on freaks who started
knitting booties in their sleep after the bad
reviews came in. Oh, I could tell you
family history, or what I ate for breakfast
and watch you furiously rearrange letters
as you drool over the prize behind the curtain.
If you made the word *SEXFIEND* or *CITIZEN*,
congratulations! Here's your Naugahide easy chair
or trip for two to the Nutrasweet Celebrity Open.
Or go ahead and take what's in the big box:
a sense of accomplishment. The hum of a refrigerator
doesn't represent the rotting produce inside.
When I step out of bed, I fear I'll fall
through the floorboards to the center of the earth.
Now how would I explain that phenomenon?
The lobes of the brain are separate,
but proximate, like twins who spy on each other
for ideas on how to live. Or let me put it this way:
Suppose I saw you inching away from the park
a stolen cactus bulging under your clothes,
could you admit that you were scratched?
If the number of letters in my name
corresponded exactly to the number
of rashes on my heart, I'd hike up my saddle,
say This is where I've been, This is where
I'm going, I'd follow myself like a sign,
I wouldn't be writing this poem.

II

Excuses

ORIGAMI FOR ADULTS

People who've seen relatives die by fire, stand
to the right of this line. People who've imagined large,
drug-taking siblings, crouch down by their feet and warm
your hands. People who offer syllogistic explanations
for plain brown acts, play musical minds to the tune
of any anthem. People who delay sobbing to answer
the telephone, people who voluntarily live in Nashville,
people who cheat by memorizing the eye chart at the D.M.V.,
march down the main street of television wearing
your tongues on your sleeves. People who've said everything
necessary in one passionate round of naked defilement,
roam anywhere, like lucky ghosts, ingesting all of the whiteness
of lies, but none of the calories. People who do
what their fathers did, people who don't believe in death,
people who never think for a minute about stepping
out of your skins, join hands. We're going to play
Pass the Broom. People who want to be heroes, lie down
as flat as roads. People for whom a Presto log
is a harbinger of desire, people whose mouths have dried up
and healed over like blisters, people who've jumped
off bridges, ecstatic, only to be rescued by stubborn
fishermen, inhabit the chandeliers and drool down
on the rest of us with Christian pity. All together now:
Try not to conciliate. Try to stay inside
your own county lines.

DANIEL

Daniel standing at the door lengthening
in the long false spring that frames him
motions me to take off my language and heed
his level country. Hamlet wiped his hands
on the world's dirty apron, but Daniel bends
like a drawbridge to tie his own shoe. For years
I have been sitting on a rusty throne inside
the Elsinore of his record collection.

Daniel is alive in the pinkest sense. His automatic
harmony is the I-beam on which I can't love.
Together we hear the splat of a suicide
on the front walk. I lie brittle and strewn
as a skeleton, though my mute blood wraps me
in silk scarves. Daniel is a hand, holding me
up to the light, shading the glare from his eyes.

Music can find feeling in the stiffest corpse,
and grace enters through my earphones'
tiny holes. Our minds burn through the pillows
of our nap— or is it a meditation?
I swallow the literature, lest I should be
hauled in for questioning. Love's laws
are elastic, it seems, but friendship—friendship
never lies. Just ask Daniel, my alibi, my
Horatio, the living proof that I'm dead sane.

Joint Venture

He never had a town or a name to shun, then later
tattoo on the bald part of his arm. The big city
sealed off his hiding place with a stain-
resistant shrug and washed its hands.
Trouble wouldn't even stick. He tried changing
his mind to see if that would make a difference,
but the bolt lock on opinion was as strong as money.
I met him in the hair-space between March
and February on the tail of a yellow light
in a big wind. He nailed me for driving
barefoot. "Ma'am, do I see what I think I see?"
A truckload of balloons struggled up
behind his head, an exclamation from the next county.
His hair swerved toward them. Primary colors
lie sometimes. I took him home and licked
the insides of his elbows and he roamed
all over me.

Opportunity is chance with a line of credit.
I was tired of blooming in window boxes, being
mowed, pruned, shorn on the first of each month.
Shuck a face and you'll find one plump kernel
willing to try anything. When the silverware turned up
missing, I made my lap a motel room, a late-night
trysting place for debutantes and rabid, ravaged
dogs. He dug in, his head in the familiar stew
of unfamiliarity, his toes on the coastline
of residence. We wear our clothes like bridges,
being mostly water. We bear the underprivileged
look of someone without real estate.
Ah, real estate, the foam in my mouth.

The Devil's Advocate Threatens the Devil

If you won't cross your teeth for me, then leave me
alone with my Apple computer. All the colleges and universities
in Toledo will bury my main points. If you won't
butter my biscuits, I know a chain store who will.

If you won't please my puzzle, I'll eat the hairdo
off your Barbie. Anyway, it doesn't matter if the moon
holds up the grass, or the pizza is pitted with lawn
chairs. If you won't tell me to my face
I'm beloved, I'll develop a comprehensive health plan.

The table breaks wherever my hand falls.
Like a kind saw, I destroy my life.
I can charm any institution.
I was born this way, a restless food in my mother's dish.

If you won't curve like a tetherball around my solar
plexus, spin like a headline into next week, dance
up my body like brand new math, cradle my howl
in your all-night kitchen, punish my agenda with your
little black prayer book, wipe my parade with your spill,
I swear I'll handcuff the fire of the future to my chair
and we're not leaving here until I get some answers.

FAIRY TALES

1

When night sprawls,
I want to feel a pink, brocaded gown
crushed and muddied under my warm,
lucky feet. Please, please.
Let me call your name and see you
turn and take off your sunglasses.
Come with me into the backyard, I want to show you
how the artichoke bush rises up to finger the hibiscus,
and how my neighbor parades around his pool,
naked, furiously pleading his case.
Tell me those aren't blue contact lenses
and that your real home is a small town in Kansas.

2

I am made of marble.
I sit perched on my grandmother's mantle
between the Hummel and the ivory banana.

CRUSH

A crush made to fit like a shoe,
pablum, a squeaker's need for an oily
plum, a glue. Why is it
with stupid people I'm in a rush to prove
I'm holy as a saw, winsome, dangerous,
and extradental, while socked in a room
with a windy mind and lips that
sew a hole right through me (cartoon critter
baptized by a cannonball, newly breezeway, gap
to fit a claw) I take myself down
like an art, Belittle, Be little, imperatives
I obey until I'm big enough to tuck
behind a molar in his jaw? Suck me,
Probe me, I'm made dumb
by neologisms and Daffy vs. Donald theories
(hyperbolic lapses and gauged manipulations,
muses both) ponying up from the ivories
of a married guy in map-of-the-world shorts.
This gash in my head, teeth set
in a dash, flesh in a world of dictionaries,
opens and closes like a cuckoo clock,
predictable as Wiley Coyote, feet scrambling
in midair, animating the long tradition
of announcing intervals.

THE PHYSICS OF DATING

Back home with Pop Tarts and brandy I refashion
the lapsed evening. No, I won't drive you back I said,
it's early and we're young and we can. Then I unstuck
her zipper and thought My Life Has Not Been Wasted
and she casually turned up like a piece of evidence.

Get me on a radio talk show and I'm monosyllabic, but
when I want to get laid I sidle my Cadillac mouth
up next to obfuscate and titillate and animal husbandry.
I'm impressed, want to take off my clothes slow and search out
that coffer of chalk talk, that fountain of youth.

Hi-oh, loneliness is a bad drug, it maketh me lie down
in stagnant waters and peel my bones dry. Tell me again why
what could've happened didn't and what didn't happen could.
Hang on to your holsters, we're going down to the shrugging
beginning of kindness, the fig leaf, the shroud.

She laughed at my jokes, then we were riding silent
with the cold. Both unknown and unknowable: right there
is the vicious, viscous paradox of desire. Even the word
desire melts in your mouth, the way the outlines
of bodies wobble and wave and won't stay put.

WARNING

Oh I'm so grown up with you, and airtight
like a citizen. My sleeves intersect
my wrists as though they would
cut off my hands. I must have worn out
two or three good suits
getting back from next Wednesday.
I never scowl or bark or roll my eyelids
inside-out. I wield the postal service
like a sword, that bright blue box
chomping at the bit, always ravenous
for new meat. But stay with me,
and I'm warning you now, comrade,
the youthing process will begin.
I'll remember things that never happened
and reenact them in restaurants.
Sandstorms will be status quo.
I'll ask you for car keys, political asylum,
candygrams, and tomorrow's weather.
I suggest you start building
that fortress now, high up in thin air,
the one you'll need when my drool
floats your house away, and my laughter
opens all your curtains.

LETTER TO JEANNE

Potato chips fly east on Washington Square
never to return to the bag. The wind
licks deep inside my sleeve. You're brushing
up your Spanish in the Pan Am wing
of San Francisco International, night flight
to Guatemala, murmuring into an airport-
priced cup of weak coffee, your stomach
already gorged and deflated. I think
you'd like this slow night in New York,
the first of winter curing whatever's habit.
I can't say there's no torture, no vicious
unkind. My cells comprehend it even when
my heart blows jazz into the eyes of every
dog or human passer-by, all of us pretending
to live by the rule of the handclasp
and the cut leash. Above me, like bodies
stacked in neat piles, the longnecked storm-
clouds of theory. I flash them my full
set of teeth. I toss a rope of cigarette
smoke up to the Seven Sisters, who live
shoulder to shoulder in their crowded house.
Sing loud when sirens pass, they advise,
and wander in this darkness with somebody.

NIGHT FLIGHT, CALIFORNIA

Night, that millionaire, invades on a whim.
Clouds stretch like taffy in the heat,
jabbed by prehistoric spirals. No one else
with a window seat goes white when heaven's
home fires burn quick down the length
of a god's skeleton-hand: orange-pink and white,
a trick of the sky, a talent. Minus the proper
musical score, an organ chord with its foot on the gas,
or one of Coltrane's famous rants. The cabin's full
of sleep and unsleep, reading lights spotting
the aisle like tall glasses of milk. And the sky
claws out again in color while the man
in the Michigan T-shirt's making a list, elbow
bobbing shadow—the mind comes up with categorical
desires a mile a minute. Even your airport words,
"Oh, heat lightning!" and your kiss like slang
won't erase the frenzied smile sparked up
inside me, a world dark and shameless,
our tiny plane dangling in chaotic space.

LILA

Lila taught me that the bones are the things that last.
Mine were hard and getting harder, whitening under the
pressure of her calculations. She was crafting me like
a mosaic, a cathedral window; every precious part of
me strained toward light. She knew what to do, how
to separate each color and then inlay, deepen, brighten,
polish with her warm wet cunt creeping up my leg like
a slide trombone, making me wait for her mouth on my
breasts, my nipples growing up toward her like seedlings
after a stunted winter, lonely faces through prison bars,
hands that need money, drugs, liquor, bread. And when
it came the heat was the heat of control, her teeth
artisans filing her metal, firing her clay. When I was
the right temperature, when I could be wrapped in glory,
when I could be trusted, and praising, and praised, she
would start to sing. Sing with her body moving against
me like a winding street. Her mouth would gallop between
my legs, her tongue a palm leaf, burning, fanning, her
teeth nicking my clit, two fingers inside me moving like
a small question. And I'd ride that horse down the street
with my hair rising up in the flaming windows of sky,
a sturdy beating pulse down a curving broadening street,
and she'd start to lose her steering, this is the best
part, her government would argue too rapidly, her blood
had more than one country. And suddenly I'd grab her
waist, flipping us over, her back pressed flat against
the cold wall, her arms flung across me like sunlight,
and I'd be the roller coaster, the carriage ride, the
bump-and-grind southern drawl guitar lick inside her
gleaming human skin. I was a flashlight in a graveyard;
she was the jewels of the dead, shining under the earth,
bitter and pissed off and taking it with her. I'd say
Taste this life, sucking the numbers from her dance card,
her ashtray, the center of her sweating nervous moaning
body. Religion is like that—just when you think you've
made a perfect prayer, the weather sweeps your house
up and your car and gives you instead orange trees.

DON'T MOVE

Don't move. Don't move at all. Let me do this.
Tomorrow you can wheel your bones along the edge
of time's illustrious curves. Next week you can make
your deliveries, manhandle your offerings, perform
your acts of contrition. Mold your vessel. Drop
your footsteps like fireflies into the void.

But now, notice your torso in flames.
The sunlight from the east rises at your thighs and cuts
the eyes from your face. Your legs lie like shadows
on the bottom of a forest, keeping their collected
secrets, burying their swollen names. I'll touch
your legs. Don't move. I'll slide up your skin
like a slow boat fights an iron current.
I'll navigate toward light, my fingertips burning
in the new world, and capsize
in the hottest part of you.

Can you hold the sunken treasure—garlands of rubies
choking your worded thoughts? Can you hold up?
Can you fight? Can you fight the urge to run?

SWAMP THING

The gravel by the road leapt
for my calves like icy fish
in a hungry cold. No streetlights.
Each curve a dare. My bare
eyes hunted the white line my bare
legs followed. Pine trees held
a literal dark inside the dark.

"Love is situational," you said,
and switched on the late movie;
Swamp Thing dripped and soared
its way into the hotel room
with a swagger that could not
be ignored. Your legs caught tight
in a sheet clench on the bed.
"I'll walk up the highway,"
I said, taking my key.

The blemished and nosy moon
pressed her face against the black
pane of sky. Panic had stolen
my stone throat and sane thighs.
The wind crouched clever, like
something unloved, then caught me
loud, a wild dog. A fierce
provision. A fast-melting half-moon

floated in your bourbon and coke.
This monster's not vengeful, just
large, like Adrienne Barbeau's
breasts in that negligee. Did you rise,
wade through the jeremiad
to wet your face or stare at your
eyes, or drift out by the tarp-
covered pool? Or, sensing
some iniquity, did you tilt up
and follow the plot? The trees

were their tall selves, and the
sounds of the generous night
made room for me, moving
apart just slightly. Fear is
situational, I thought. A promise
made to oneself can't be broken
by someone else. A car barked
and swerved when I caught
its poor headlights. Your hands,

bony and knowing and so
unaware, dangled in my mind
like bait. The blue light of
innocence hummed in the distance,
masked by trees, but I knew
it was there.

I Still Dream of the Taste of You

I still dream of the taste of you,
musty-sweet as a rare book,
field smoke brushing a night train.
Kisses mouth of pink oasis, fruitful
and whiptorn, carved from rose stone.
Quick and sure, like a thumbprint, your love for me.

My dreams frightened you: your body
the bed for a waterfall, landing place for all
fearless, dislodged things.

A river has no color, except for what holds it,
above and below.
Were you scared of what you might do?
Start to need me? Turn to rock?
Break the backs of fishes?

Notes from a Visit with M.

A hero is a dead person, full of rattle.
A hero doesn't pace or yawn or divide.

You walk from the sink to the refrigerator,
a giraffe casually looking for food.
Drunk, your hexagons lurch but don't spill,
the path between them temporary as land.

Stars keep appearing at the wrong house
so I chase them down the unlit street
and herd them into clusters. I'm a shepherd,
a wallet, a turnstile. The end of the line
is nothing but a muddy embankment.

What happens to a gift that can't be given?
You wave coffee over the bed and want to know.
A practiced gesture, like a tongue
that keeps returning to a blooming tooth.

TRAVELOGUE

I walk in a blue wind.
Eggs crack and yolks fall around me,
bobbing belly-up in the hard afternoon.
Don't guide me, I see
how that path muddies.
In the wobble of human desire,
I'm constantly improving my dodge.

Two bald-headed girls find each others'
mouths, fumble and score, backed against
a pool table, thwack of the break, their scalps
hatch and sing.

Each day I grow more convincing:
Muses shaking hands inside me need me,
feed me. I'm an incubator, a cardboard box
slashed and duct-taped, rattling
on a conveyer belt. I'm
the conveyer belt.

One thing I'm not— I'm not
spoiled by love. Stick a finger in me, I grip
like an anemone. Underneath my softness,
rock. Wedding-dress white and
calcium-carbonate bloom, I walk.

LIBERTY

I'm in Philadelphia
for no reason!
I'm in concert park
without a mouth harp.
The light of a serious skin
leads me by the collar
and buys me breakfast.
There are no circumstances,
just the outlaw joy
of walking north to south
on streets my feet discover.
Fuck cancer today.
Fuck love and longing and sex
and waiting for the light to change.
Birds glaze buildings
with the sweet mint of flight
and boxcars skulk
in the switching yard.
Lucky pilgrimage claps
its hard-earned hands
above my head
while a Hammond organ
rides by on a flatbed.
Horns bray at the sun, large
like a country, tame
like a country. Dusty
and blessed by the cool arms
of history, I tumble out
where the Delaware River
is a big calm flood
born before Ben Franklin
or Betsy Ross, and the
stomach greets moonrise
with a turkey sound,

a question instead
of an answer.
Clouds of insouciance
that sparkle and groan
in the watery slate-smooth
backdrop of time,
Clouds of Philadelphia,
be there
when they cut open
this bulky heart.

Natural History, New York

There's Theodore Roosevelt with his natives,
begging for a mocking glance. From up here,
he can look down his nose at the moon
that barely made it to the fifth floor
on the east side. It's that number of the night
you can trust to welcome you with jumping
garbage and graffiti police, when the puckered
sky socks in your wildest dreams of sleep,
that time when you can boldly be
both Ethel Merman and Donald O'Connor in duet,
when green Jupiter shakes off his oily rags
and dances a slow ferocious dance.
Behind these brass doors, the plastic
vertebrae of dinosaurs' broad backs
glow in the protective hum-light of history.
It's too late even to pay lip service
to the idea of going to work later; a shower
wouldn't look good on you yet. The hard seeds
of fatigue fan out inside you and
imbed themselves, little religions.
Oh how you want to be in that number
when morning spins around the earth like a dial
on a telephone, leaving its small sudden flame
glowing behind the screen door of each town,
like this one.

Escape Plans

No money or business being tabled.
Think I'll go to jail and get wrung
out, shuffleboard on the deck, firecrackers
every night in the yard, don't look nobody
in the seat of their pants. It's a classic
routine, this wide tread mark, I've seen it
in black and white and primrose and still
I point my finger at the thing not to it,
bleed all the bank accounts down to a combed-
up pompadour, beat the million dollar question
to the starting gate, where the cleanest,
barest truth seems purloined
and minute. Behind bars, every world-
scented postcard would be more than none.
And promises, good old promises to the self,
would be tubular and sturdy, such as one
might whisper through, instead of old
family recipes to be thumbed apart
and sternly chewed.

Rockabye

Strange hotel, this beachside cradle, winds
warmer than sing-song and gritty, slime sand
sucks me in its mouth, buries me to my chin,
cool caress and alien, under the tongue,
the jurisdiction, of the sea.

My real mother's a wet blot on the skyline, deep
and going deeper. She's given up on terra firma;
her red maillot bobs and eclipses like a stinging eye.
The sun shrinks us and we're charms on the bracelet
of this coast's long wrist.

I extract one gluey foot, behold
the messy ladder of the underworld. I'm gripped,
though, unborn. Curled around a heartbeat, both blessed
godchild and gagged captive, I swim in the belly
of the beast, bang on the gate in that calcium light.

This place eats females, I've seen it.
So far out now, she's no more than a splash or a puff
of smoke briefly interrupting the seascape.
Cliffs soak up bright spray, wide-necked. Surrounded by curves,
everything in me wants to erect.

OKLAHOMA

In the wild and silly West, my mother visited me
from death. We sat on a peeling wooden bench
five feet back from the forever tracks, dust
wearing the land like an old monkey fur, hot
wind slowing down time. Her gloved hands, her
buttoned boots, her pigskin valise. Awnings
that shaded us from love. The five o'clock train
howled from practically Texas, throwing its
rumble down the smooth metal arms that reached
beyond our feet. Change, change. The body
of noise passed close enough to touch, and you
were in her place. Your grin rode high on your
face. I tell you, I liked you from the very first.
When you kissed me, my mouth could be any shape.
I didn't know sadness from happiness, or how many
limbs we had, wheat stalks waving like mad, or
who was feeding whom. All our disappointments
were on the lam. The sky was the color of sand,
the stretch and tenor of brindled sand. My
bed rocked and woke, my hands tucked in, warm
skin folded my own swells and curves, and taking
in the dawn marks I baby-cried for another room,
wider and incurable, despairing of a tender
ear, a listening womb, a lover west and south,
a railway transfer bending time, a breast
in the mouth.

GRACE

I don't know anything about Grace. I just like
the sound of the word, how it bandages the elbows
of sentences, bolsters the thin sheetrock
of chin up and a smile for everyone. The sheer
prowess of the capital G, its fiducial curl,
inspires in me a kind of Pavlovian panting: suddenly
I want to have a heart, to take an oath, to
doodle furiously in the branches of a family
tree, to bestow a secret handshake on the beautiful
sylph who just crash-landed in my strategy.
Her eyes have lengthened beyond my
horizon. With smelling salts, I fashion my S.O.S.:
"RESEMBLE ME."

Maimonides struggled toward Providence, which is like
retirement, only upper case. Anything studied
becomes prodigy: typing, walking, speaking in tongues.
Sure, teeth are miraculous, but who has to
cut them? And hair—God, hair—is secured
for a firm price. Life. What have I done
to deserve this? Paddled upstream with a meal
in my mouth. Said things I didn't mean.
Danced with the rector's illegitimate son.
Something for nothing is a bedtime story
problem I was never told. I've seen Amnesty follow
on Crime's heels. Grudge buries the hatchet
between Grace's eyes.